RISE TO THE TOP

Coaching Insights and Challenges for Leaders

Julie L. Compton, PhD

Rise to the Top: Coaching Insight for Leaders
By Julie Compton, PhD
Copyright © 2019 by Julie Compton, PhD, and JC Learning

For further information about executive 1:1 coaching, speaking engagements, professional consultation, special bulk pricing, or other related inquiries, see the author's website at www.comptoncoaching.com.

Cover Design: 99 Designs
Editor: Kim Foster

ISBN: 978-0-578-45763-5

First Printing
Printed in the United States of America

What Executives and Thought Leaders Are Saying About Rise to the Top and Working with Julie Compton as Their Coach

"Ben Franklin advanced the thought that the best teachers are the ones who make you feel you are not being taught. This is an amazing read told through a captivating story—a plane-flight read packed full of lessons for leaders at all levels. Julie has provided a blueprint for leaders, as well as coaches."

~ Phil Harkins, Author, Thought Leader, Executive Consultant, and Coach

"As my coach, Julie spent the necessary time to learn my strengths and improve areas using modern tools and techniques and developed an action plan to make immediate impact. Julie had the courage to speak truth about my situation in a way that was clearly intended for my development. Her work is not limited to management and leadership growth; she evaluates the whole person to ensure proper balance in every aspect of the leader's life necessary for maximum performance."

~ Greg Randolph, SVP of Global Sales, MobileIron

"This book is an essential guide to leadership! What makes this book truly special are the coaching challenges. The questions/assignments are practical and relatable. All one needs to do is open their mind for honest self-reflection and do the coaching challenges. Julie is a tremendous coach and the first person to help me understand my triggers, how to influence, and how to manage key stakeholders. She changed my life both inside and outside of the office."

~ Missy Schnurstein, Head of Product Marketing and Demand Strategy at Verizon Media Group

"Julie has been in the trenches, and from those valuable experiences comes this sage advice for leaders. Follow the practical wisdom she offers, and you will get better as a leader of teams."

~ Thomas G. Crane, Consultant and Author of "The Heart of Coaching"

"I can relate to Dianne's career story portrayed in *Rise To The Top*. Many leaders are consumed with inner doubts about their abilities to lead a team or company effectively. After all, it's extremely lonely the higher up an organization you travel. Julie's book provides insightful thoughts, lessons, and challenges that assist leaders to be more effective. I learned a valuable lesson that leadership is about who we are and not governed by what we do. As my coach, Julie created a scope of work to evaluate my current status, identified areas of improvement, and generated a comprehensive plan to achieve our agreed goals. She is a consummate professional. I would highly recommend her to any individual or company."

~ John McCulloch, Global Vice President, Current Business Owner

I dedicate this book to my beautiful, strong daughter—God gave you the power to lead and make a difference in this world. I am proud of you and blessed to be your mom. Go girl!

Contents

Introduction:
Why You Should Read This
Book and What to Expect

WHETHER YOU WORK IN business, nonprofit, or education, if you are *leading* or *coaching* people, you will relate to this story. You may have faced similar scenarios and challenges in your own leadership journey. So set aside some time to disrupt yourself and gain insights and actions you can take from this book to be a more effective leader and coach.

First things first: let me introduce you to Dianne Gableton, a strong, successful woman who never planned on becoming a CEO, let alone being celebrated for her achievements. As you get to know Dianne, you'll encounter a few of the leadership lessons she has learned as she transitioned in her career. This is a "cut to the chase" story to captivate your attention and draw you into quick learning as you relate to Dianne. Each chapter progressively follows her career from a college graduate to becoming a CEO. There are many lessons in her story for both coaches and leaders.

After you read a portion of Dianne's story, a nonfictional section that relates to one specific leadership insight will follow. There are 10 main insights. Each insight outlines current ideas on the topic, including suggestions and actions from your coach (*which is me*), and thought-provoking questions to help you dig deeper and learn more about each leadership skill or attribute. I encourage you to take the time to reflect and apply the action items at the end of each chapter. If you do, I guarantee you'll coach yourself to raise the bar on your own leadership capabilities.

I have been working as an executive coach, organizational consultant, and leadership facilitator for over 23 years. Prior to that, I worked in business and in academia. One thing I have seen repeatedly is that most leaders face the same learning opportunities and difficulties along their journey. How you show up as a leader and whether or not you continually learn and change are what make the difference! I know this book will provide you with numerous insights for those learning opportunities.

1. Today

THE ALARM IS RINGING again. It's disorienting after a long night working with my team. Who even invented the alarm? It's such a loud noise interrupting my deepest, most peaceful state of sleep. Even with the iPhone's calming Calypso chime, the abrasive intrusion demands that I haul my butt out of bed. Some days I wonder, *How can I still be creative, productive, and lead from the front when my day begins this way?*

My temporary moodiness melts away the minute my feet hit the floor. As usual, I head for my latte and start getting excited about what the day will hold. Then I remember—and I begin to smile—today is the day I've been hoping for my entire career!

2. Twenty Years Earlier

"Pearls don't lie on the seashore.
If you want one, you must dive for it."
—Chinese Proverb

I WAS 21 YEARS old. College flew by in the blink of an eye, and no one—and I mean *no one*—was going to stop me from achieving my dreams and all that lay ahead. It was a stereotypical ceremonious day: an inspiring speaker, hats tossed high in the air, and parents proudly hugging their graduates. Most college grads agreed they felt inspired because they had survived their college journey. Listening to the speaker served to further inspire and motivate them on to greater achievements.

"Are you Dianne Gableton?" asked a tall man wearing small, wire-rimmed glasses. He proceeded to look me over as if assessing me. "It depends who's asking," I laughed boldly. I was in the zone and feeling very successful.

"Well, that depends on if you're Dianne." Without any hesitation, he had easily matched my tone. Pausing briefly, I took the leap and responded, "Yes, I'm Dianne."

I felt exposed, like I was putting myself out there with no idea of his agenda. It was as though we were in a chess match and he'd just claimed, "Checkmate!"

"Well, in that case, if you're willing, come with me. I want to introduce you to your employer." Employer? Now that was odd. I'd turned down every offer I had received over the last three months throughout the college recruiting process. To be honest, I had found them all very boring.

"There must be some kind of mistake," I voiced quite adamantly. "I haven't secured a position yet."

He looked at me and very slowly said, "Well, it's up to you. But I honestly believe the mistake is about to be yours if you don't follow me." He pointed me in the direction of a big, black limo that was sitting in the roundabout, apparently waiting for me. I stood there for a minute, pausing to look back at my friends who were all laughing, hugging, and reminiscing. For a moment I was almost lured back, but something inside, like a sixth sense, stopped me.

"Who are you?" I asked. He handed me a card, and without giving it another thought, I took a step toward the stranger and my future.

Lesson: Risk

*"The biggest risk is not taking any risk.
In a world that's changing really quickly,
the only strategy that is guaranteed to
fail is not taking risks."*
—Mark Zuckerberg

LEADERSHIP REQUIRES RISK, AND risk is inherent in everything we do. Risk is essential to innovation, improvement, and sustainability. Exceptional leaders must always be aware of the level of risk required in specific situations. Leaders need to be able to determine whether or not an action, decision, potential product, or path is the right one. After you've done your due diligence and reviewed all your options, you're left with only one thing: to calculate and measure the risk and make a decision. Risk management simply helps us make better decisions.

As a leader you have to be fully aware of your own bias, both toward or against risk. What drives your bias? What are the indicators of too much risk? What signs suggest you aren't taking enough risks? Think about it: all quality financial planners include risk models in their planning, professional surfers calculate risks before committing to a big wave, and fashion designers know the risks before launching a new design.

No profession is without risk; some risks have bigger pay-offs and bigger fallouts than others. So, how do we assess risk? Many leaders would say it's about listening to your "gut" or intuition. Listening to that inner voice begging to be heard. Exceptional leaders acknowledge this voice but only while also employing logical and analytical tools to calculate risk. So yes, listen to the voice but also use your intelligence and tools to make a decision.

What are those tools? Here are a few ideas: gather and analyze data to determine risk; look at people who have gone before you and made similar mistakes or successes; calculate the ROI of the risk; reach out to consultants and seek diverse opinions. You can apply risk models, read books on the subject of risk analysis, hire a coach, or meet with a mentor. Whatever methods you choose, stay open to outside ideas other than your own. There is such a thing as balance. You want to avoid becoming too much of a risk taker, or on the flip side, of becoming a leader who shies away from risk. Know yourself well enough to know how you work best and, in turn, how to maximize your tolerance of risk.

You might also face career opportunities that require you to take a risk. As an executive coach, I have watched many individuals struggle with decisions on career advancement, changing organizations, and overseas opportunities. These decisions are tough and should be well thought out. What is right for one person may not be right for you.

For example, I coached a woman who had made a job change within the same large, retail organization every two years or less. She was well respected for her problem solving and her deliverables in the different functions she had worked in. At one point she was asked to interview for a position in merchandising, which would be entirely new for her and she could potentially fail. At the same time, she had an additional interview for a position she knew she could excel in, but it would not provide the same level of learning or exposure.

We discussed her long-term career goals and her current family needs, along with thinking through what it would take to succeed at either job. She ultimately decided on merchandising. She was up for the challenge because she was willing to do whatever it took to succeed. She knew the short-term sacrifice would have the long-term payoff for where she wanted to go in the company.

Coaching Challenge

As your coach, I challenge you to do the following:

1. Think about a risk you took that worked out. What were the contributing factors that ensured its success? Now, think about a risk you took that didn't work out. How did you go about analyzing both decisions? Was there something different about the risk that worked out? What can you learn from the decisions you made?

2. What is your overall view of risk? How could it possibly impact your career?

3. Given this reflection, what are you considering doing differently in your leadership, business, or life today? What is the risk? What are you going to do differently to confront that risk?

4. Check out some risk management models that include risk identification, risk analysis, and risk response planning and monitoring.

3. The First Months on the Job

"Leadership and learning are indispensable to each other."
—John F. Kennedy

I SAT PROUDLY BEHIND an oversized glass desk in front of the largest office window I have ever seen in my life overlooking the city. *Mind you, I hadn't really seen much at my age.* I tried to hide my excitement. To be honest, my elation felt a little immature and unprofessional. But there I was, an associate in a major startup company who—through the help of some risk-averse investors—had become successful almost overnight. *Me!* An account executive at one of the top-10 startups. This company had even earned an award for the best place to work in my state.

I was the envy of all my friends and the main topic of conversation at my parents' social parties. And to be honest,

I felt this job was a bit over my head. I wanted to pinch myself, but of course I hadn't admitted that to anyone. In fact, I was scared to death they would find out that I wasn't capable.

Every once in a while I'd hear this little voice suggesting they had made a mistake and it wasn't going to last. It wasn't that I lacked confidence in my ability to learn or to execute, but I was unsure of the business world and how to navigate my way in it. It seemed I had everything I needed to succeed in my office; everything I could possibly need to do my job was at my fingertips. I had the latest computer equipment, virtual reality meeting rooms, and access to any building on this beautiful, expansive campus. I was responsible for one of the largest new accounts we had just sold—seriously, it was the business deal that was going to sustain our future. And you know what? That account was my idea!

As a student, I had become friends with Justin, an innovator extraordinaire. It wasn't his handsome face that drew me to him; it was the way my excitement grew when he talked about artificial intelligence and the convergence of the Internet of Things. I felt intrigued and excited when I was around him. He was different from me, yet I knew we had many things in common.

When I landed this position, he was the first person I thought of contacting. He fit our company profile for clients we wanted as partners. Little did I know, Justin's company would end up signing on, and it would be the *biggest deal* in our company's history. To top it off, my manager suggested I be put on the new account—I was *thrilled*.

Now there I was, only 30 days into my position, as the adored newcomer who brought in the big fish, but somehow I still didn't feel like I had done anything. It's sort of like when you think you missed the mark with a dessert recipe and everyone thinks it's incredible, or when my friends were in awe over my renovated house, which seemed to me to be so easy to do that anyone could have done it.

I'm not sure why I struggled with internal doubt. Others said I needed to believe in myself—to see myself the way other people saw me. But here's the thing . . . I *did* believe in myself. It was just that it was so easy to get there that I felt like I must have been a fake, or that I was missing something. Maybe I was not as good as people thought. Of course, my brother kept telling me, "Enjoy it," and "Don't worry about it! Unless you do something wrong, you're solid." I *wish* it were that easy. My brother's advice didn't get rid of that nagging, doubting voice inside.

You may be thinking I had low self-esteem, but it definitely wasn't that. I did believe in myself, trusting that I'd win; it was just that deep down inside I felt like I didn't know enough to be where I was and have people's respect. I wished I had a better handle on exactly where that doubt came from and what caused it. Every time I was handed something, I executed it like a charm. I received accolades, but inside I questioned if I really knew what I was doing. My brother called it being a poser. "Dianne," he said, "that's not you!"

It wasn't like I managed people or anything—now THAT would be amazing. I wasn't sure I could even *be* a manager. I felt comfortable maintaining the account and overseeing its growth with a little help and mentoring from others. I knew I could compete in that part of the organization, but I wasn't sure if I could do anything else.

Lesson: Competence, Humbleness, and Managing Our Internal Dialogue

"Everyone must be quick to listen, slow to speak, slow to become angry."
—The Bible (James 1:19)

MOST OF US NEVER really know exactly what we are doing when attempting something new, until we work hard enough at it to master the skill. Sports is a great analogy: it takes years of training, repeating the same exercises over and over again to create muscle memory, reactions, and the timing to be a master at whatever sport you choose. Ask all the greats, from Michael Jordan to Peyton Manning: repetition, repetition, repetition. We learn from our mistakes. Habits are formed over time.

Noel Burch developed a learning model that suggests we are incompetent and unconscious about what we try in the beginning.[1] Over time and with repetition, we gradually move up the ladder to become consciously competent and finally, unconsciously competent. The journey is similar with most everything we undertake. No one is born with great parenting skills or management abilities, or can even compete and win a bike race without learning and repetition.

Once we've learned something and feel competent in it, it's important to claim that attribute or skill in a humble and authentic way. We all have different levels of comfort with our abilities, talents, and knowledge. In the early stages of our career, it's normal to feel doubt, question ourselves, and perhaps even be overly humble and not take enough credit. Once we start receiving feedback from our team, customers, peers, and managers, we begin to solidify our perception of self.

There's a crossroad at some point in which we have to "own" our abilities and successes instead of downplaying or dismissing them. It doesn't mean we take credit for everything; in fact, we become better at sharing the credit with the team while remaining confident in ourselves as leaders. Leaders either tend to give too much credit to their team at the risk of not being perceived as capable or involved, or alternatively, leaders can take all the credit and alienate the team, being perceived as egotistic and boastful.

Later on as we progress in our careers, some leaders are challenged to remain humble. Often, I run into leaders who believe they should have a certain demeanor and level of arrogance in order to be perceived as a competent executive. This couldn't be further from the truth. There are many great leaders, such as Mark Bertolini, past CEO of Aetna, who are very strong capable leaders, confident yet humble in their approach. Other leaders have strong, demonstrative egos to show they are in control. Usually they are hiding behind a protective barrier or are unaware of the internal fears they wouldn't dare show. Other leaders demonstrate their inappropriate ego through nonverbal communication, aggressive tendencies, or always trying to be the focus of the room. Gathering honest feedback to determine how you are perceived is the best way to stay in check of your own ego. Just make sure you ask those who will be honest with you.

There's a reason why it's "lonely at the top." There are many expectations for higher-level leaders. Once you are at the top of the ladder, there are few "safe" opportunities to discuss concerns, fears, and your own internal dialogue.

Managing your internal dialogue is a must! It's a necessity no matter what your level of leadership is within an organization. Experience, age, culture, and many other factors contribute to how you form your self-image and present it to others. And although no one else can see or hear your internal dialogue, it has a deep impact in every way on you as a leader.

Your internal dialogue manifests itself in many ways: through facial expressions, body language (e.g., slumped shoulders, eyes rolling), and your tone of voice. How do you show up to others? Your internal dialogue might be saying to others, "I'm not good enough," or "Why would they believe me and what I have to say?" Or "How can that person be so stupid!" Whereas, to the other extreme, your inner voice might suggest, "I'm the expert here. Nobody else knows as much as me, given my experience," or "They couldn't have done it without me."

We all have an internal dialogue to manage. The theory of emotional intelligence (EQ), made popular by Daniel Goleman,[2] helps us to understand how to manage our internal dialogue. One of the four components of EQ—*self-regulation*—specifically relates to managing our dialogue. If we're aware of our inner dialogue and we're able to control and adjust it as needed, we are displaying high self-regulation. Self-regulation of our emotions, thoughts, and behaviors isn't always easy, especially when we are "triggered' in the workplace by people and events that connect with our history and personal baggage.

One of my clients had a perfect example of this. Every time she walked into an executive leadership team meeting, she was reduced to short sentences and often never spoke up at all. This change in her style was noticed by her peers, but no one ever gave her any feedback. Eventually, she gained a reputation in the meetings as someone who didn't speak up, and therefore she didn't receive her next promotion. Through coaching, she recognized that the executive vice president (EVP) of human resources (HR) was the individual who triggered her quiet demeanor and feeling of intimidation. In fact, we went back into all her prior interactions with the EVP to sort out what had occurred and where she could start changing the tapes in her head.

Of course, we all take our humanness to work every day! I encourage you to dive into understanding what triggers you and learn how to alter your thoughts, develop new scripts, and embark on new techniques for self-regulation.

Coaching Challenge

As your coach, I challenge you to do the following:

1. Think about what you're good at and whether or not you "own" your skills and abilities in a respectful, humble, authentic way.

2. List your strengths and the areas that you struggle with. Decide on actions you can take to practice and master those skills.

3. List common, internal dialogue statements you consistently say to yourself—good or bad. What do they tell you? What affirmations and positive statements can you use to replace those negative thoughts?

4. Challenge yourself to show up differently. Pick one thing you would particularly like to work on, and focus on this skill for the next 10 days in a row. Doing this will give you an opportunity to be aware of yourself and to see if you're committed to changing your habits.

5. Check out the book *Triggers*, by Marshall Goldsmith, listed in the recommended reading section in the back of this book.

4. One-Year Anniversary

"Great stories don't always appeal to logic,
but they often appeal to our senses."
—Seth Godin

LAST WEEK AT THE executive leadership meeting, I had to present a strategy for doubling sales revenue through our partnership with another company that is sometimes a competitor. It was the first time I had presented to executives. Keep in mind, nowhere in my MBA did we receive advice for the mental preparation needed to knock it out of the park. We'd only learned about creating PowerPoint decks and the basics of delivery.

Now, I admit . . . I was a good presenter, but presentations at this company were at a whole different level. I'd watched other people present and always believed they had great storytelling skills to draw people into their point of view and convince others. I wished I had that ability, but where could I get it? It wasn't like purchasing ice cream at the grocery store. You know, when you have that sudden craving for Ben and Jerry's ice cream, and you just go to the store and buy it!

I was honestly feeling some angst, just knowing that I hadn't prepared enough for this presentation. Of course, that was when I heard them call my name. They were running ahead of schedule. "Dianne, would you mind going next? We've had a change. As it turns out, Tom won't be here until later, so we'd like to start with you."

"Of course!" I said, trying to swallow the lump in my throat and calm the nervous butterflies in my stomach. "Thank you all for coming. As you know, we're trying to . . .," and "one potential solution is . . ." "If we did A . . . then B . . ." "I recommend . . ." And of course, to wrap up, "Are there any questions?" Umm . . . BORING!

You know when you realize something didn't go as planned? Well, I knew this was nowhere *close* to some of the presentations I'd seen from others. However, at least I included all the facts that supported my point of view. I was happy with myself for doing a good job of putting my data out there.

Once the meeting was over, I asked my manager for feedback. He started by asking me a few questions. First, he asked if I had considered adding storytelling or influential language to my presentation. Sheepishly, I replied no and proceeded to explain that I didn't really know how. My manager was very helpful and pointed me toward resources that would teach me about those skills. "Did you talk with any of the executive leadership team ahead of time *about* your presentation?" he asked me. No, again, was all I could say. "In some instances," he stated, "it is important to socialize your ideas prior to presenting in order to gain some buy-in and also to hear objections others might have."

Fortunately, my manager was supportive. Somehow, he saw through my protective demeanor and strong façade to the trepidation I sometimes felt, though he never said it to me directly, which was fine by me. His advice was *exactly* what I needed to hear.

In the future, I would remember to socialize my ideas, network with others, and get their reactions *before* a presentation. While he himself was not good at it, he knew enough to encourage me to get better at socializing my agenda.

As I walked away, I was *determined* not to have an "average, at best" presentation ever again. I didn't shoot for mediocrity.

Lesson: Influence and Preparation

"People buy into the leader before they buy into the vision."
—John Maxwell

To INFLUENCE OTHERS—THROUGH PRESENTATIONS, meetings, or a 1:1—you have to think through your influence practices. Who do you meet with regularly? What is your primary influencing style? How do people view you? How specific are you with what you are trying to accomplish? How well can you articulate your view?

Influence is about bringing others along into your viewpoint. It's not coercion, nor intimidation, nor even political power. It's not convincing others to see what you see; rather, it's a collaborative approach in exchanging viewpoints so yours is clearly understood and accepted. This takes conscious effort.

One gentleman I coached was highly admired for his ability to influence others to see his perspective through the art of asking questions. In a way, he was leading others to his point of view, while creating an atmosphere of collaboration. He did it authentically, however, while listening to others' perspectives. His skill in inquiry and advocacy was noticed by all stakeholders that I interviewed, so much so that his managers asked him to leverage his skill in the "art of influence" by teaching others in the organization how to influence.

So where do you start? First of all, you must establish relationships with the right people to be able to influence them with your ideas. If you've taken the time to build stakeholder relationships, the foundational trust you have established will give you an edge up in credibility, as well as having their ear. If you're trying to influence others who don't know you, it's much more difficult to persuade or convince them because you haven't established trust.

Second, be selective with the words you use; language will impact how the listener receives your message. Four of the main influencing styles are reasoning, directing, visioning, and collaborating. Adopt these styles to drive positive interactions with others. Although there are various models of influencing, they all have something in common. Each method requires the ability to flex/adjust your style to the other person. The other two influencing styles are inspiring and asserting, according to a *Forbes* magazine 2010 study.[3]

Another major component in getting buy-in to your ideas is *when* and *where* you influence. Like anything else, there's a right time and place. If your idea is tough or complicated, make sure you're meeting with individuals in the morning, when the majority of people are at their best, mentally sharp and recharged. Afternoon meetings on the other hand tend to find people restless, struggling to concentrate, and sleepy.

Think about how you can use the room or location to your advantage. For example, people are usually more open to ideas when they're not at a work campus or building. Use nonverbal cues wisely, tell interesting stories, pay attention to your body language, give applicable examples loaded with data, and incorporate colorful language to tap into others' emotional preferences. Tailor your message to different audiences.

In my coaching practice, I often find leaders don't prepare nearly enough for conversations that matter, such as presentations or developing specific arguments for their point of view. In fact, most leaders run from meeting to meeting only thinking about what they're going to say in the brief moments in between. Of course, they're not unique in this—we're all guilty of it. Overscheduled, ruled by the "tyranny of the urgent." But I urge you to keep in mind that the more there is at stake, the more time you should prep. You want to avoid giving off any negative impressions while presenting your deck. Practice in the mirror—look at your facial expressions and what you do with your hands; look for how you can show confidence, and rehearse it. People think it is all about the deck, yes, and . . . it is about you!

Your language choice may be the difference between the acceptance or rejection of your ideas from your peers. It takes practice and self-realization to effectively prepare specific conversations or presentations in advance.

Coaching Challenge

As your coach, I challenge you to do the following:

1. List the stakeholders who have the power to impact your ability to get things done, along with those you need to build trust with. Who will you need to support your ideas in the future? Meet with someone you need to establish a better relationship with.

2. Make time on your calendar to meet with those individuals in a *SMART* (specific, measurable, achievable, realistic, timely) way.

3. Practice an influential style (visioning, reasoning, inspiring, collaborative) you might not have used in the past. Try different techniques and figure out which one works best for you.

4. Seek feedback in the next 30 days from a manager or peer you trust regarding your presentations or even how you show up to others.

5. Evaluate the purpose of your presentation. Is it to present data only or to present a specific point of view to influence others, or both?

5. Another Project!

"As all entrepreneurs know, you live and die by your ability to prioritize. You must focus on the most important, mission-critical tasks each day and night, and then share, delegate, delay, or skip the rest."
—Jessica Jackley

THE LAST SIX MONTHS were so exciting! Especially since I was promoted to manager, overseeing a team of six people within the newly launched, consumer-driven product. I had the opportunity to manage the P&L globally, which was new for me, and take responsibility for developing new markets with my team. I'd taken on a lot of work recently. It became apparent when I noticed my calendar was booked 7 a.m. to 7 p.m., and my daily running time was suffering. If I didn't arrive at the office at 6:00 a.m., I'd never get my emails cleared out. Everyone told me it was part of moving up in the organization, but I found it all a bit overwhelming.

I had been at this company almost two years, yet I still felt like there was so much to learn. I didn't want to turn down any invitation to work on a project.

I shared this with a trusted coworker, Lisa, a peer who worked with a similar-sized team in a different division. She had about five more years of experience than I did. Lisa had always had my back since day one, and I counted on her now and then in a casual mentoring relationship. It only took her about five minutes to get to the bottom of my concern. She coined it as "delegation," and I termed it as "fear." She told me most of my responsibilities were really for the team to bear—not for me to do it all.

"In fact," Lisa stated, "you are keeping people from growing by doing their work for them." It was something to think about. I thought I was delegating, but maybe my team was capable of more. Maybe I needed to adjust what I was working on.

Upon reflection, if I were being honest with myself, I was a bit fearful to let go of certain tasks, just in case my team didn't do a good-enough job. Lisa encouraged me to read a couple of books on delegation, and then sit down and see where I could start letting go—not just for my sake, but for the development of my people as well.

Lesson:
Delegation Matters

"Don't tell people how to do things; tell them what to do and let them surprise you with their results."

—George S. Patton

WHEN MOVING UP THE ladder into management, *everyone* experiences the transition from being a task-driven, individual contributor to managing others' workloads and learning to delegate. And let's not kid ourselves—it's hard to learn how to delegate. One way to think about it is by using the 5-W and 1-H question technique. Ask yourself: *What* are you needing to delegate and *why*? *Who* should do it, are they ready, and do they have the knowledge, skills, and time? *When* should you hand it over to them, and what expectations should you share with them? *Where* will you get involved to coach them along the way. *How* will you make sure they are completing it to your satisfaction?

Some leaders look at delegation as just managing the workload. It's actually about developing people, getting the most out of their talent, and developing their capacity to be the best they can be. It's an opportunity for those under you to learn, grow, and get better at what they do. Without delegating to others, you also get stuck in your day-to-day, which leaves no time to influence others or work on strategy.

In addition, you need to hire the best and then let them own their work. Your employees need to be *empowered* and learn what it's like to be pushed. You need to be OK with letting them make mistakes. Pick situations in which they might fail so they can learn but won't be making mistakes detrimental to the company. Coach them along the way, and this will reduce your fear. This is the fear that most managers have when it comes to letting go of the work.

You're not alone if you have a difficult time delegating. According to the Institute for Corporate Productivity (i4cp), "53% of 332 polled companies have a 'somewhat high' or 'high' level of concern about the time management skills of their employees, and 46% of the companies feel the same way about workers' delegation skills."[4] My work with leaders across multiple industries supports this statistic. Although individuals are putting in more hours, the demands are greater between technology and multiple tasks vying for our attention.

Brian Tracy, renowned expert in productivity stated, "The average person today is working at 50 percent of capacity. With effective management and delegation skills, you can tap into that unused 50-percent potential to increase your staff's productivity."[5]

When a leader delegates, it also fosters a future network of champions and supporters. Teams that are strong due to their leader's delegation, coaching, and interest in their development end up as strong cheerleaders for their manager. Often, teams who are successful can propel a leader forward into greater job opportunities and recognition. Don't underestimate the ability the team has in making or breaking your career and your reputation.

If you are focused and clear in the work you are doing, you will delegate more appropriately. Greg McKeown, in his book *Essentialism*, gives us three core truths that support this: "I choose to," "Only a few things matter," and "I can do anything but not everything."[6] These truths can guide us in our leadership practice. Being able to say no to all things that are not essential or core to our roles frees us up to pursue what matters most and allows others to maximize their talent, bringing clarity to their purpose.

Coaching Challenge

As your coach, I challenge you to do the following:

1. Take an hour to complete these five steps:

   a. Sort your work and your team's work by priority.

   b. Then sort again into "who" should be doing it.

   c. Ask yourself what would happen if you didn't do what was in your stack and someone else did. What is the obstacle, fear, or issue you have with delegating it?

   d. Pick one of your responsibilities and begin to train/coach someone else and practice handing off the responsibility.

   e. Apply the 5-W and 1-H question technique for delegation mentioned at the start of this chapter.

2. Think about what is essential to your job and your success. What is your unique capability that you bring to the position? Are you maximizing your strengths? In what way would your team benefit if you did?

6. The Team Grows

"Great companies don't hire skilled people and motivate them; they hire already motivated people and inspire them."
—Simon Sinek

I'VE NOTICED SOMETHING ABOUT time—besides never having enough of it! As in business, all things change and *keep changing*. My team was large now. Through a series of promotions, I now had 12 direct reports and 52 indirects. Sometimes I felt disconnected from my team, but really, we were performing well, making our numbers, and meeting all quarterly objectives. Even better, my department and team had received the company award for innovation! I *loved* my job and enjoyed going to work every day. I had come to understand I was motivated by making a difference in both the company and the team.

I realized my position was changing and so were the company's expectations. I used to conduct skip-level meetings once a year, but my agenda was so full that there was little time to meet anymore. I trusted my direct reports to let me know if something was wrong below them. I had an open-door policy and tried to touch base now and then with my down line to find out how things were going. I regularly conducted a weekly team meeting with my direct reports, and I was sure if there were issues, they would come up in those meetings.

It had taken me four years to reach the director level, and it felt great to excel in my position. I was confident and comfortable with my skills and my team, and I was capable of handling the conflicts that happened every now and then. My peers were usually supportive; however, I had one peer—Franco in manufacturing—who was particularly difficult to converse with. He acted like he had all the answers and constantly interrupted people. Up until that point, he'd never gotten in my way. I basically tried to ignore him and stay out of his way. That was all about to change.

I overheard one of my direct reports, a manager I counted on, Matt, talking about the lack of motivation among some of his team members. I remember being a bit surprised—I'd thought everyone on his team was functioning at their best. I invited Matt into my office one day to talk about what was happening with his team. He didn't readily open up or share any concerns, which surprised me because I thought we had a fairly close, trusting work relationship.

Toward the end of our conversation, I mentioned how I'd overheard him discussing his team's lack of motivation. I could tell he felt a bit sheepish and even surprised as he looked down at the floor. Matt sat down and started sharing, "I wasn't sure I should tell you."

When we got to the bottom of it, it turned out that a handful of Matt's team members were totally disengaged, and as a result, the production in manufacturing was slowing. It was barely noticeable, mind you, because we were meeting our goals, but the prevailing attitude was spreading quickly. It wouldn't be long until it started affecting the bottom-line results in my department. Matt was hoping it would resolve itself if he somehow worked harder, but it didn't. After some prodding, he admitted he should've come to me earlier to discuss this. He thought since he was the manager, he should be able to handle this without me.

It took us quite a while to get to the root cause of the attitude of his team. It turned out it was a combination of two things: first of all, Matt's team saw him as being egotistical. He repeatedly told his team what to do instead of involving them in the strategy and discussion. Matt was not known for developing his people. Therefore, team members were not feeling motivated to be a part of the larger company initiative. Instead, they felt like only task deliverers.

Second, there was a disproportionate amount of influence on Matt's team coming from my difficult peer, Franco. Franco had been bypassing both of us and going to Matt's team to get what he needed. Franco was head of engineering, and when he did not get his approvals, he took matters into his own hands. Matt's team was in need of some immediate help. We had to turn things around before it got worse, or our positive results were going to decline and people might leave, resulting in high turnover rates. In addition, it was obvious—I would have to deal with Franco.

Lesson: Engagement and Building Effective Teams

"The ability to establish, grow, extend, and restore trust is the key professional and personal competency of our time."
—Stephen Covey

THERE ARE MANY KEY elements to building effective teams and not enough time to cover them all here. To begin with, you must commit time to meeting with your team. Knowing how often to meet with your team members individually and as a whole is key, and it will be different for every company and with every team. There are so many variables that shape the dynamics: time, projects, accessibility, culture, norms, trust, and individual styles. Even if you've set up the right number of touch points with your team, you can still sometimes be surprised and things can happen, catching you off guard.

I once coached a CEO who thought he knew everything about his executive team, especially since they met regularly. They worked together to set the vision and strategy for the company. He thought his team trusted him. He thought they would come to him when needed.

One day, one of his employees came to me and told me in confidence that he was afraid to share with the CEO some crucial data because it would either change the company's direction or potentially lead to its demise. When I asked him what his fear was, he became visibly nervous and fidgety. It was obvious that even though he worked with the CEO every day, he didn't think the CEO would believe him. He worried that he was at risk of being fired if he was seen as having an opinion contrary to that of the CEO, even if he thought his information was pertinent. The employee had seen this happen to others, which was part of what made him hesitant about speaking up. At the same time, he knew he had to share his perspective for the good of the company.

Creating a safe place for people to speak up is imperative for leaders. Employees can fear their managers, even if it's just due to their title. So as a manager, even if you think you've built a solid relationship with your employees, don't be afraid to look a little deeper for what might be getting in the way of open communication with your team.

Employee engagement requires both individual attention and organizational assessment. Most of us have been a part of a company-wide culture engagement survey at some time, and usually we have the same complaint: "What's the point? We give the feedback and then nothing changes, so why bother?" Leaders need to implement actions that will shift the culture or influence others who have the control to do so in the organization, especially after a survey has been completed and the results are in. The worst thing you can do for team engagement is to participate in a survey and then not respond.

Leaders also need to ensure they are taking care of their own down line when it comes to engagement. Engagement begins with knowing your employees. Do you know them personally? It is not about having to invade their private lives. Instead, think of it as being interested and caring about who they are as people.

In addition, you need to know what motivates your employees. Are they altruistic, money-oriented, socially motivated, or achievement driven? Perhaps they desire recognition, pleasure, or flexibility. Many of our motives are not so easy to see, while others appear more obvious.

Next, you can connect your employees' motivations and values to the organization's mission and why the company exists. A study by Tiny Pulse found that only 42% of employees actually know their organization's vision, mission, and values.[7] Do you know your bigger *why*? Do your employees? TED Talk guru Simon Sinek is so obsessed about the why that he wrote a best-selling book on the topic, *Start With Why: How Great Leaders Inspire Everyone to Take Action.*

Are you as a leader connecting your employees' motivations to the bigger picture of the company, project, or future state? Stay close to your people, keep the lines of communication open through regular meetings, coaching, and living out the example you want them to follow. Your reactions to all incidents and situations set the tone for how much information your employees share with you. Your actions and behaviors teach employees whether or not they can trust you.

Trust is the most essential ingredient for successful relationships, and it needs to be built with a conscious intent. We all know that trust takes a long time to develop with others and can be easily broken. Stephen Covey, author of *Seven Habits of Highly Effective People*, stated that trust is like a checking account—for every withdrawal you need seven deposits.[8] Spend time "depositing" in your team's and peers' accounts. You need to be other-focused in order to build trust.

There are different models of trust in business literature—however, the key elements of most models include being competent, credible, reliable, and communicative. Your character says so much about you. Look at the rise and fall of many famous people, such as actresses, sports stars, and politicians. Often, it is due to their character. What does your character say about you? Make sure your actions indicate you're trustworthy. Display traits such as following through, being authentic, and being dependable.

Coaching Challenge

As your coach, I challenge you to do the following:

1. Start engaging your employees in new ways, such as projects or new initiatives, or helping them master a new craft.

2. Read a book on engagement, such as *Multipliers* by Liz Wiseman and Greg McKeown, and implement a new action.

3. Ask your team to be a part of the planning process or strategy session.

4. Write down what you value in each employee and make a point to share it with them this week.

5. Practice active listening in order to look for your employees' motivations and understand who they are as individuals. Ask them about their motivations if you cannot pick up on what they are. Then brainstorm how to value your people and schedule activities that will tap into their motivation. Remember to update your calendar with the activities.

6. Take an assessment to understand your own motivations.

7. Communication at Its Best . . . and Worst

"Listening is an art that requires attention over talent, spirit over ego, others over self."
—Dean Jackson

As SOON AS I could get on his calendar, Franco and I sat down for a cup of coffee at one of our campus cafés. At the advice of my mentor, I picked a busy, outdoor café, as I thought it would be neutral enough for both of us to stay open-minded. I chose a public place because Franco was known for raising his voice.

Conscious of my dislike for Franco and his undermining action of going behind my back to the team, I knew this wouldn't be an easy conversation. I realized I had a tendency to judge fairly quickly if someone challenged me and I held onto my perception for eternity, even if someone tried to change his or her behavior (something I had been working on after I learned about it from one of my work-style assessments I took).

Sadly, I had never considered building a work relationship with him. I saw him in meetings all the time, but he always dealt with my manager, not me. In retrospect, that was a stakeholder relationship mistake on my part. The conversation may have been totally different or perhaps not even required at all if I'd taken the time to connect with him previously. I was done beating myself up for my mistake, and it was time to deal with the conflict.

Franco arrived late and was in a rush, as usual. With niceties quickly out of the way, he was ready to get down to business. He seemed genuinely surprised at my request to meet to discuss the project interaction between my team and engineering.

"So, what did you want to discuss?" he asked, taking a sip of his coffee while watching people passing by. I thanked him for coming, then tried to apply a communication technique that had worked well in other situations: *state the situation, describe the behavior, and ask for what you need.*

"Franco, our teams are not working well together. My employees are feeling demotivated, and I am concerned about our numbers. I believe you have been frustrated with our process and have gone directly to employees rather than Matt in the past. Would it be possible if you went to Matt first?"

Immediately, Franco blurted out, "Well, I don't see that happening at all. Since Matt is never around, your team needs more direction, and I stepped into that gap. They don't understand time lines or our design need. I merely provided what was missing."

Now, my heart was racing. My approach generally worked, but not in this case. His interruption was too much for me. I asked him, "Can you please hold your reaction until I can finish my thoughts?" He looked at me doubtfully, as if I had already shared my thoughts. He was impatient and I reacted, visibly annoyed.

"Look," I said, "Matt is doing a great job working with manufacturing. We haven't been late on any deadlines, our products are to spec, and response time to your needs is all within reasonable timeframes. I would appreciate it if you would bring all of your concerns to me and I can coordinate with Matt." That seemed to make Franco angrier, and he raised his voice.

"I don't have time to find you every time to run my ideas through you and also clear what I need from your team. I need immediate access when there's a problem. If Matt could actually handle it, I would go through him, but obviously he can't."

Oh, boy. This is not going to be easy, I thought to myself. I took a deep breath and remembered something else in the back of my mind—wise advice: listen to the other person's needs before sharing your own.

Intent on a good outcome, I sat back in my chair and started asking questions. "What is happening when you go to Matt? Tell me the issues between our teams. What is holding you back?"

It wasn't long before he started to cool off, and I understood the bigger picture from his point of view. While I didn't agree with everything he said, I did hear him out. I remained quiet about solving the issues and instead shared the impact he was having on our team by going directly to the team and not through Matt.

I remember what my mentor Lisa had told me: *"Listen first. Give others a chance to talk. Do not resist, defend, or debate. This only raises resistance. Try to build bridges of understanding."* I think I did a pretty good job following her sage advice. In the end, I bought the coffee, knew we had made progress, and learned I needed to stay ahead of him in the future. Franco was one person in our company who could benefit from learning new communication skills. I knew I couldn't change him, or even give him feedback because he wouldn't take it. However, through this interaction, I learned more about what was *not* working about my approach!

Lesson: Communication and Conflict Skills

"Most people do not listen with the intent to understand; they listen with the intent to reply."
—Stephen Covey

ONE OF THE BIGGEST challenges for a majority of people in the workplace, and in life in general, is communicating through tough discussions and conflict. Many leaders come to me for coaching to explore the difficulty they have engaging in dialogue with somebody with an opposite point of view, especially when they don't get along with the person. Typically, leaders are aware of issues that arise due to the business agenda. What's harder to figure out is *why* we have issues with other individuals and *how* it affects us, therefore impacting the business. A majority of my clients have at least one person who somehow "triggers" them. Once we're triggered, our basic self-control and communication skills disappear.

What are the most important skills required for effective communication in the workplace? Every leader thinks they communicate well, but 70% of my coaching engagements with senior leaders involve learning new habits, or changing mind-sets about people and forming new patterns. You've been exposed one way or another to the basic skills of communication, so I don't want to repeat them ad nauseam; however, some foundational skills are worth repeating: *listening, empathy, inquiry,* and *advocacy.* They seem basic, but be honest. Are you really using them? Here's a short recap.

Listen to others, and by that I mean *really* listen, not just to the words coming out of their mouth but also to their body language, their facial expressions, and tone. Look for the entire message and then practice summarizing what was said to you back to the person. This affirms to others that you were listening and heard them, and it creates the impression that you value what was said, even if you disagree with them. Listening ends when you know what they said and understand them from their position (which is what empathy means).

Only after listening should you respond with your comments or questions. This very important skill is often missed due to many factors, including today's global world pressure that creates a time crunch. Not to mention that some individuals are very task-oriented versus people-oriented, and diverse individuals process information in different ways and speeds.

Inquiry is asking questions in a variety of ways to probe, confirm, challenge, and understand. Using inquiry is the best method in influencing others to see your point of view. It also demonstrates listening to and interest in what another person is saying. Using inquiry with others allows for creative ideas to emerge and creates an atmosphere for healthy debate.

Edgar Schein, in his book *Humble Inquiry*, took questioning one level deeper by suggesting we need more humble inquiry, defined as "the fine art of drawing someone out, of asking questions to which you do not know the answer, of building a relationship on curiosity and interest in the other person."[9] I couldn't agree more. Why is it so difficult to master this ability? I believe, like Edgar, the task-driven world we live in does not support the culture nor the time it takes to slow down and show interest in another person. Telling is much easier than engaging in a dialogue of curiosity.

The opposite of inquiry is advocacy—sharing your point of view in a way accepted by others. In conversations, you can either push people into your point of view (which often produces defensiveness) or pull them in instead by the use of advocacy and inquiry combined.

Adopting an attitude of curiosity will help neutralize conflict situations. My esteemed colleagues Michael and Curtis helped me drive this home for a participant when the three of us were facilitating a leadership workshop for a major oil company. In the middle of the workshop, one of the participants began to vehemently argue about a concept we were presenting. My colleagues and I stopped pushing out the "wise" advice and moved to a place of curiosity about his point of view, shown through entering the participant's world. We did our best to demonstrate interest and inquiry and come from a genuine place of listening. It wasn't long before the individual retreated from his anger and moved into a conversation. Eventually, we were able to bring the conversation back around to the original ideas, and the discussion was productive.

Another area leaders tend to fall short in is communicating well in 1:1 meetings with direct reports. Choosing to listen, inquire, and set expectations clearly creates an environment for trust. In addition, motivation and empowerment are couched in these conversations.

All 1:1 meetings should have a coaching approach, unless it is clearly a performance conversation. The motivation for the leader to have regularly scheduled individual meetings is for accountability and sharing of information. The main result for the employee is enhanced motivation, a feeling of being valued, and connection to a greater collective purpose. If intrinsic motivation is what it takes for individuals to be creative, engaged, and productive, having these 1:1 meetings taps into their needs. Leaders must make this a focus if they are to succeed in today's tight labor market and constant need for reinvention.

If you tend to downplay the value of your people as compared to your products or services, take notice. A recent study by Korn Ferry Institute on motivation stated, "The value of people within organizations—their ability to lead, to create, to drive change—is 2.33 times the potential of assets like technology, real estate, and inventory that are the focus for most companies."[10]

Coaching Challenge

As your coach, I challenge you to do the following:

1. Think about a person you are either in conflict with or you don't have productive conversations with. What would be the impact to you or the business if you changed that relationship? What do you need to do to begin?

2. Discover your own bias through reflection, assessments, trainings, or working with a coach or others.

3. Make it your goal this week to be "present" with others. Let listening be your guide. Write your goal down in your meeting journal or on a sticky note, and practice summarizing back to others before you begin vocalizing your own thoughts.

4. Think about how you can establish and maintain a position of curiosity with those who seem to irritate, annoy, or oppose you.

5. What is your commitment to regular 1:1 meetings with your team? How can you create time for your team and value your people through this process? Write down the results you notice and track the meetings' agendas. Make sure you only take up 20% of the airtime during the conversations.

8. Am I Connected?

"The future depends on what you do today."
—Mahatma Gandhi

I WASN'T SURE I had time for it, but I received an invite to the Leadership Circle, a six-month intensive training for high potentials. The training was part of the culture, and quite frankly, also an expectation if you wanted a VP position. I loved that the program included self-assessments, as well as coaching sessions. But how would I fit it into my busy schedule? I was thrilled at being invited because it showed they were taking me seriously. My feeling of confidence increased when I realized they recognized my talent, and I definitely wanted them to! Certainly I would attend and hope the training wouldn't get in the way of meeting my business objectives.

I'd been considering leaving the company if I couldn't attain the VP position I wanted. Five to seven years was a long time to stay somewhere; most people move on every three years, especially if they're not being promoted. I felt

I had a fantastic opportunity there and knew I served the company well. I was ready to move to the next level. When I told my manager, he responded, "After your training, we'll see what the reorganization does for open positions." He was pretty supportive of me; however, I think his boss, an EVP, didn't think I was ready.

My last 360 highlighted a few areas I needed to improve, such as coaching with my team and becoming known in certain circles within the business. I had put some effort into improving those areas, but I still had a lot more to do, especially in the area of coaching. It was an expectation of all our managers now, but it wasn't the case when I was hired.

Matt was scheduled to meet with me that week to discuss his promotion. I needed to think about how I would explain his need to develop himself and his coaching skills. Given that I still needed to work on my own coaching skills, I wasn't quite sure how to go about having that conversation.

I also believed I hadn't been visible enough for the EVP to even notice my improvement. I was relying on my manager to channel that feedback up.

I decided to meet with my mentor, Lisa, and talk through my current concerns. When we sat down for lunch, I told her, "I think I might be getting stuck in my position, but

I'm not sure. I need to develop my coaching skills as well. What do you think?"

Lisa began by asking about relationships I had with others in the organization. How often was I meeting with others outside my area, who was my champion, and how might I get more visibility with my manager? I'd never really thought about *intentionally* connecting with peers and upper-level managers; I'd always just worked with whomever I needed as work unfolded. I realized it was time for me to put a plan together to meet more stakeholders, so I committed to Lisa that I would and booked a time to meet with her in three months for accountability. We also discussed how I might improve my coaching skills and my direct reports' coaching skills at the same time. I was very thankful for Lisa. I hoped one day I could mentor someone as well as she had with me.

Lesson: Stakeholder Management

*"The most important thing a captain can
do, is see the ship from the eyes of the crew."*
—D. Michael Abrashoff

IN MY COACHING PRACTICE, almost every client engagement I have includes a conversation about stakeholder management. Good stakeholder relationships across the enterprise are imperative for VPs and EVPs—you should begin developing them early in your career. Even if you're just starting out as a beginning manager—whether your vision is to climb the ladder, be the most impactful leader you can be, or sit on an executive team—having solid, trustworthy relationships is foundational. If nobody outside your inner circle knows you, then when the time comes to gather support or work with others, you'll have a harder time because you're basically an unknown.

Take time to build your reputation and connections intentionally and early on. Begin with asking yourself the question: *Who are my stakeholders?* They can include people you meet with regularly who impact your work, those who might be obstacles in completing your work, leaders you need on your side, or individuals who could be valuable for a future promotion.

One of my clients who worked at a software company thought he had great stakeholder relationships, until one day when he needed buy-in and support for a recommendation on how to move forward with a big change that would impact the organization. He spoke with me about how shocked he was that others outside his circle of influence hardly gave him the time, let alone be influenced. When I asked him to describe his relationships, he realized he had rarely met with them and didn't actually know much about them, other than hearsay and a few casual hallway conversations in the office.

Leaders need to think ahead and manage their relationships. That doesn't mean any interaction should be fake or manipulative; leaders need to be forward-thinking. Begin by thinking about the outcomes you want, then work backwards to think about the people who will need to be a part of the process along the way. There are also external stakeholders, those who are outside of the company and need to go through the same rigor.

Relationships are the foundation of work. If you don't develop them intentionally, they will still develop, but by default, which means you'll end up with others perceiving you not as you intend. As I always say when I'm facilitating a leadership workshop: tasks get done by people. Put your focus on the people first, and the task will be made easier.

Coaching Challenge

As your coach, I challenge you to do the following:

1. Conduct a stakeholder analysis: list people you need to meet with who impact your career, your work/projects, and those you need to influence. Prioritize the individuals and begin with the most important.

2. Block off time in your calendar to meet regularly with your stakeholders. Make the focus about creating a relationship. Be careful not to avoid the people you're uncomfortable with or whomever you're facing conflict with—those might actually be the most important stakeholders to meet with.

3. What are you doing to build trust with others? What have you done in the past to create mistrust? Who do you mistrust and why? What can you do to change that perception?

4. For more insight into creating a network, read the article, "Stakeholder Management" by D. Ogwell (refer to the recommended reading list in the back of this book).

9. Career Choices: My Horizontal Move

"Opportunities don't happen;
you create them."

—Unknown

IT WAS TIME FOR my performance review. I went in prepared to ask the hard questions to determine what I needed to do to get the promotion I desired. I wasn't surprised when my manager shared his plan for me to take on more enterprise-wide projects. He offered a horizontal move that would allow for greater visibility and help me learn more about certain parts of the business outside of my area, all while managing a bigger team.

I was excited, although somewhat disappointed that I couldn't move straight into a VP position. I knew if I succeeded in this new role, I would be in a prime position for a promotion to VP, so I accepted the offer. Having such a large team meant I had to rely on coaching my direct reports more effectively. A lot of the workload would need to be moved downward. Just in the same way as I struggled previously, many people below me weren't delegating enough.

I met with my mentor again. "Look at it as leading people, not just managing their workload," she said.

It got me thinking, and I realized that my entire management team needed to improve at coaching. I decided to have them attend a coach training session. I knew about an external consulting company that had done a great job within our organization and felt the cost would fit my budget expenditure. Besides, it was heavy on the practice of coaching, not just the theory.

Once the training was over, I noticed my team's reluctancy to apply their new coaching skills. When we got together to talk about it, people expressed their concerns about the drain on their calendar. It took time—you had to be patient, ask your employees questions, and wait for them to solve their own problems, instead of jumping in to "save the day."

Matt, who had been struggling to get promoted in part due to this very issue, was the exception to the rule; he actually embraced the approach. I think it was because he was really ready for change. I was thrilled to see his style develop over time, and mine had improved as well (I believed we could always improve at anything we tried). As a coach I took the time to ask my reports about their work—what they'd done, what was difficult about their situation, what they'd tried, and a whole host of questions before I just jumped in and fixed it for them. I wanted them to feel empowered to make decisions and develop their skill sets.

I faced some pushback from people who preferred I jump in and solve their problems, but over time they either got on board or moved on. Now that I was coaching more, I had more time to innovate, strategize, and influence across the organization in my new role. I was excited about the chance to learn more through my exposure to other sides of the business. I was determined more than ever to be a senior leader in this company and impact the business. What an exciting opportunity and major responsibility— and I was anxious to be there.

Lesson: Coaching Your Team Works

> *"Before you are a leader, success is all about growing yourself. When you become a leader, success is all about growing others."*
>
> —Jack Welch

IN THE 1990s, WHILE living in San Diego, I designed and rolled out a training program for a corporate pet retail store intended to develop coaching skills in their managers. The design was fairly innovative at the time and resulted in managers opening the lines of communication and empowering their employees. It took another 10 years for "coaching skills for managers" to get traction in most companies. In today's organizations, coaching skills is one of the top-five delivered programs in learning and development. If your organization is not managing with a coaching style, you're losing ground to your competitors.

It's not that other styles aren't needed, such as directive, collaborative, or consultative—they are all valuable. They each have their time and place. The primary reason for the rise in coaching is due to the VUCA (volatile, uncertain, chaotic, ambiguous) world we operate in. Business is moving exponentially fast, and innovation is key for survival. There's not enough time in the day to stay abreast of all the trends, let alone continue to adapt our competitive position and remain strategic. We need to constantly develop our employees and leverage their strengths to stay competitive.

Coaching develops your employees to think for themselves, tackle tough challenges, and be accountable. If you coach your employees more often, the natural result is an increase in the bottom line. Not only are managers more effective, but it frees up time for the higher-level activities that often get lost in the day-to-day management and execution of business: activities such as strategizing, planning, innovating, and having time for challenging debate.

Allow me to briefly describe the coaching approach used in most organizations today: the GROW model developed by John Whitmore[11] in the '80s. He believed in unlocking people's potential to maximize their own performance, helping them learn, rather than teaching them. The acronym GROW stands for goal, reality, options, and will. The fundamental idea is that during a conversation, one person will walk the other through this model by asking open-ended questions, so the other individual will arrive at their own solutions.

Begin by asking, "What is the issue or goal?" Then assess the current state or reality of the situation. Next, explore the options, and last, look at the commitment(s) that can be made by the individuals. This model is a good framework, but it doesn't teach someone how to coach. The underlying intent of every coaching interaction is to build awareness, responsibility, confidence, and self-belief in the mind of the coachees, empowering employees to find their own answers.

Most of the industry uses coaching in two ways: developmental coaching and performance coaching. The purpose of developmental coaching is to enhance employees' abilities, skills, knowledge, problem solving, and decision-making. It is great for periodic check-ins and reinforcing new skills. The GROW model can be effectively applied here. Performance coaching, on the other hand, uses the GROW model as its base, and in addition, the manager adds more directive or descriptive language to point out a performance problem.

Here is a simplified common scenario: a manager tells an employee their work product is subpar and would like to have them change their performance. The manager shares with them the specific behaviors or problems. In this case, they are missing details on their reports and providing incomplete data. The manager opens up with describing the goal of what the work product should look like and explains the current state to identify the gaps. Then the manager begins to ask questions about what happened, working through the model—not necessarily in a linear manner—until there is an exchange of ideas. The manager and employee reach an agreement at the end of the discussion about how future work should look and what it takes to get there.

There are many other components for good coaching sessions, such as being trustworthy, which was discussed in the previous chapter. No matter where you build your coaching knowledge (books, trainings, certifications) just know that practice over time is the only way to form the habit of coaching and feel comfortable with the approach. It feels quite foreign at first and takes extra time. It is well worth it, especially because employees are empowered through coaching versus giving them the answers they could figure out for themselves.

Coaching Challenge

As your coach, I challenge you to do the following:

1. Determine what your strengths are as a coach. What areas need improvement? What are obstacles to coaching your employees more often?

2. Watch a YouTube video or TED Talk demonstrating an actual coaching session. Make sure it is a managerial coaching demo, which looks different than the approach of a life or executive coach.

3. Assess your current style through an assessment, working with a coach or attending a training.

4. Work with another manager and hold each other accountable for becoming coaching managers.

5. Block time on your calendar for 1:1 coaching sessions.

6. Participate in on-the-fly coaching by asking questions instead of giving answers.

7. Develop a list of questions to use and have in front of you. Practice using the questions on virtual calls.

10. Nothing but Change

"When you're finished changing,
you're finished."
—Benjamin Franklin

THERE COMES A DAY when you wake up in the morning and realize you're in a place where something needs to change. One week, I took some time out to reflect on where I had been and what my vision was for my career moving forward. I had spent many years at this company; in fact, I grew up here. I loved the people, the business, and had succeeded in my role. I was in my late 30s, had an MBA, a family, and yet, I longed for more. I first noticed the desire to become an EVP when I received my promotion to VP. I was interacting more with the EVPs working together in meetings—which, by the way, were often full of conflict, and not the productive kind—and mixing with them at different functions. At times, I thought that I could do a better job than a couple of them.

Perhaps I was overinflating my ego, but the more I watched them interact, the more I became convinced I could succeed in that role. My manager had since moved to a different company. He'd hit the ceiling with nowhere to go, and I didn't want that to happen to me. I decided to make a bold move and ask about an EVP promotion.

The feedback was unsettling. My new manager, who was highly political, knew better than to disappoint me with a "no way in hell" answer, but reading between the lines, that was exactly the answer I got. It wasn't about my performance; it was that the people in the executive suite weren't going anywhere, despite the conflicts among them. She made it clear that the organization couldn't support a newly created position because of the slower economy and the projected decrease in revenue.

I knew our organization was in the middle of a critical process of transforming certain parts of the business to stay current, and I was hoping that working through this disruption could be part of a newly created role for me. I was, after all, without a doubt one of the best innovators in the company! Our product development hadn't kept up with our pace of success (we were relying on our current stellar products), and now that the competitors were on our heels, with the risk they could likely overtake us the following year, there was a real sense of urgency.

I had a tough choice to make: Should I stay in the organization and help lead it through the waves of change brought about in our industry from my same position? Or should I secure a new job? It would have to be a lateral move to a VP position in a company with similar technology. Once I was hired and learned about their products, my goal would be to move on to an EVP role.

It wasn't an easy decision. It definitely kept me up at night, not to mention the countless hours of pondering. There were days I still wondered if I could keep putting in the hours, knowing I was giving up time with my kids. At least my weight had not changed too much, thanks to the onsite gym at work. Five a.m. came early each day, but it was worth it! I can't imagine how I would have burned off stress and stayed calm without some type of workout. In fact, I made quite a few connections with people in my industry and networked with executives of local companies during the early gym hours. It wasn't that I wanted out of the long days; I just didn't want to put out all that effort and not get promoted.

There was also a part of me that was angry, but I didn't realize it until I met with Lisa. At yet another of our 7 p.m. happy hours, I told her how disappointed I was not to be at the EVP level yet. "Could there be some reason I am unaware of, or are certain people preventing me from getting a promotion or a new position?" I asked.

As we talked, I noticed a bit of my resentment. Lisa responded with a few comments that pushed me out of my comfort zone around entitlement and personal growth. To be honest, it wasn't really what I wanted to hear. She explained that the way in which I faced obstacles and disappointments along my career actually revealed my character. I will never forget when Lisa declared, "You have been lucky not to have had too many hurdles so far. At the same time, when you've run into challenges and roadblocks, your resilience and attitude have made all the difference. At some point, all leaders face difficulties in people, their career, or life circumstances which give them an opportunity for personal growth and refinement. How can you look at this as an opportunity to improve who you are?" Lisa always came up with pinpointed questions to make me think.

I never really thought too much about my character as a leader, or how I might have needed to change myself or adjust my attitude. I was bright, accomplished, and technically sound. I managed others well and was respected within the organization. I thought that was enough. Lisa suggested I look into getting an executive coach. At first, I thought this meant she wasn't interested in helping me, or maybe she thought I might fail, but instead, she explained that successful, high-potential candidates were often given a coach to prepare for transitional moves.

So, after talking with my mentor and my family, I decided to hire an executive coach and stay at my company, helping lead it through this tumultuous time. My manager agreed to the coaching contract and understood its value. I viewed this as an opportunity to work on myself and make a few changes in my leadership style that I knew would prepare me for my next role. I was also well aware of the challenges that lay ahead for our organization, and if I managed them well, I was sure it would give me industry-wide visibility and hopefully a position as an EVP. I would need to bring my A game, giving everything I had to get this organization to pivot and embrace the changes that were underway, even if they weren't necessarily popular.

Lesson: Managing Change in Yourself and in the Organization

"Culture does not change because we desire to change it. Culture changes when the organization is transformed; the culture reflects the realities of people working together every day."

—Frances Hesselbein

LET'S START BY TAKING a look at organizational change through John Kotter's model. His classic approach has helped countless organizations implement strategic change and is still used today. The methodology consists of eight steps outlining the important elements of change: (1) establish and drive up the urgency for a need to change, (2) build a team dedicated to change, (3) create vision and goals for change, (4) communicate change needs, (5) empower staff to implement changes themselves, (6) create short-term goals, (7) maintain persistence, and (8) make changes permanent.[12]

Perhaps your organization has a different approach they prefer to implement. Whatever approach you use, I highly recommend you follow Kotter's main ideas and apply a formal approach to adopting change, integrating it into all business practices and program designs. Involve the key stakeholders from the top down to the individual contributor level. It should inform the organization's strategy and be based on a realistic assessment of the history and readiness of the organization.

However you approach change, the important and most mistreated element when guiding an organization through change is the people. I repeatedly watch organizations conduct a town hall meeting and send out a company-wide email to introduce a change. Then what? They send a generic follow-up email when the change is well underway and another one near completion, which they consider to be "communication" and "involving" people in change. As human beings, we all want a say in what happens with us, around us, and to us. An email doesn't cut it. Involvement means gathering ideas, listening to concerns, and considering the impact of change on people. Those are all important, so why is it that so many executives shy away from involving their employees? Many are concerned about opening up the proverbial can of worms; there is a concern that employees will bring up issues or ideas the managers may be unable to address or issues they've already made a decision on.

I caution all leaders to understand: successful change is *not* about creating a strategic plan in isolation and then introducing it to the team or organization. For example, in the mid-1990s, I worked with an Internet security company looking to reorganize their engineering group. The current state was stalling projects and creating a lack of communication. The three heads of the department collectively decided on a new structure and hired me to help with the rollout. My suggestion was to put their design in their back pocket and instead have a half-day workshop to present the problem to the entire group. Then they could break into smaller groups to brainstorm and come up with solutions for a report-out at lunch. I had to alleviate the concerns the executives had around giving too much freedom or saying no to proposed solutions.

Once all the ideas were presented, many of the groups came to the same conclusion. The execs incorporated many of the employees' ideas into the new design. We went back to the group to present the new structure and gathered their concerns about the rollout. The timelines were communicated at every step of the way, feedback was gathered, and people were involved. The execs still maintained the final decision-making power, which at times made some people upset. But overall, the changeover was overwhelmingly positive and met with little resistance. In fact, many new ideas emerged as a result of the employees' input, which otherwise would have been missed altogether.

Now, of course, this example doesn't fit for every change initiative, nor for every organization; however, the important takeaway is to think through the human element of the change. Make sure you start at the top and involve every layer of the organization, communicate the message repeatedly and in various formats, and assess your culture for a baseline and then at certain milestones as you progress.

While this book isn't about how to work through your own personal challenges, I would be remiss to skip making a brief point about the need for managing change in yourself. Leadership is about influencing others and having followers, but if you don't have an acute sense of self-awareness and a capacity to make changes in yourself, it will be hard to be a successful leader. You might disagree with me and cite Steve Jobs, Apple founder, as an example. He created and led his company to be the innovative giant it is today without a lot of regard to how he treated people. But frankly, I see him, among a few other geniuses, as the exception. We *all* have personal issues and carry baggage.

I passionately believe that leadership is more than leading a successful team, product, or company; it's about character, competence, and trust. A leader who is followed for who they are, not what they do, is the highest level of leadership one can attain. It's not an easy path.

Perhaps you can name a few good, leadership role models you know in either the public eye or your circle. Having an individual you are inspired to be like is a valuable way to stay focused on your own development. One of mine is a woman named Chip who helped me get started as an executive coach and organizational development specialist. Her ability to notice herself in all circumstances and choose the higher path when faced with obstacles was unnerving. She was talented, smart, and never avoided the tough stuff in her life. Chip learned how to recognize her own response to change—be it personal, external, or forced upon her. She was aware of what her triggers were. These reactive patterns from previous experiences unconsciously show up and get the best of us through actions we later wish we didn't take. She managed herself, as well as her environment, in order to minimize triggers.

If as a leader you are willing to do this inner work, it naturally attracts others to want to follow you. From an EQ point of view, you would be displaying all four EQ components successfully: self-awareness, self-regulation, social awareness, and relationship management. Most of my clients who do the gritty work on understanding themselves and the situations or people that derail them will speak about the huge difference it makes in their ability to work with people and their overall success as a leader.

Coaching Challenge

As your coach, I challenge you to do the following:

1. Make it a priority to have a change process in place. Socialize the process and begin using it. Otherwise, contact your HR or learning and development team and investigate the current change model.

2. Pick a current or future company initiative/project in which you need to incorporate change theory. What are you doing or not doing to get people involved? How are you delivering the vision to people for engagement? Where are your touch points with people? How are you working with resistance?

3. Spend time reflecting on meetings or experiences in which you communicate well, as well as times when you blow it. What do you notice between the two? What might you do differently next time?

4. Find avenues to increase your self-awareness, such as taking assessments. I like *Strengthfinders 2.0* by Tom Rath or my personal favorite, *The Five Love Languages* by Gary Chapman. Although it is a personal book, not business, it sheds insight on our main need as individuals: love. (See the recommended reading in the back of this book.)

11. A Lesson in Strategy

"The essence of strategy is
choosing what not to do."
—Michael Porter

HAVE YOU EVER THOUGHT you were ahead of the game, only to realize that you were not only behind but actually going down the wrong path? Let me tell you, it's not a good feeling. One of my toughest days at work was when I took a huge risk I felt I had to. I recommended to our executive team that we drop the direction we were headed in and instead pick up speed on a product we had decided to put on hold. I had to convince them this was the course of action to take and why.

Their reply? "No one in our field is headed in this direction. It's too big of a risk. The marketplace isn't ready."

These were only a few of the comments made at the off-site. I told them this was the moment that would make or break our organization. The room was split about 50/50 for and against. If it weren't for Franco—yes, he was *now an EVP* leading the engineering/manufacturing business—my plan wouldn't have gotten the votes it needed.

Franco and I had connected very well over the last few years as a result of my conversation with him years ago. I had made an intentional effort to keep up with him and his ego. I didn't know for sure that my efforts were the only influence that had produced the change in our relationship, because I had also heard he had hired a coach. He could see my vision, and he knew I could execute. I worked hard to create a strategy that would be well-timed, detailed, and focused on the right things. The strategy needed support from a couple key outside partners, and only two executives had the relationships needed to pull it off. I leaned on them to foster those partner agreements and spent countless hours talking with all stakeholders, consistently sharing the vision, fixing the issues, and ensuring engagement and execution through our people.

At one point, a few of my peers challenged certain aspects of my strategy. I was tempted to dismiss their comments, but I knew that everyone's perspective mattered. I was about to make or break my career on this, so I decided I needed help. With the support of HR and a verbal yes from my manager, I interviewed and hired another executive coach. We worked together in a way where I felt supported and challenged at the same time. I was able to discuss my concerns about making huge mistakes in my decision making at this point without fear or recourse—it was a safe place to have intense conversations. I also discovered what I needed to move forward with a strategy. What a difference six months made working with her!

The executives took the risk, and we put very thoughtful milestones in a timeline that would allow for a turnaround in case we couldn't execute. I believed in our strategy and our market differentiation, but I didn't realize just how much my career depended on it at that moment.

Lesson: Strategy and Execution

"Test fast, fail fast, adjust fast."
—Tom Peters

MANY LEADERS FIND IT challenging to be truly strategic, especially when transitioning up from a mid-manager level, where overseeing execution and task completion is the main job requirement. Positions at higher levels in an organization demand the ability to think strategically and keep up with global trends and industry development. In major transformations of large enterprises, leaders focus on devising the best strategic plans. To succeed, they also must have an understanding of the human side of change management (as discussed in the previous chapter). The saying in business is "Culture eats strategy for lunch." The strategic plan is a crucial element, but without translating its value through the collective actions of people, it's just a document.

What does strategy look like? Tim Armstrong, past CEO of Oath (Verizon-owned Yahoo and AOL), built Oath for the mobile consumer economy. That was his strategy. Oath's future landscape pictured consumers having access to everything they needed via a mobile platform: video, shopping, and so on.[13]

There are many ways to define strategies. I am an athlete and often use different adventures as analogies for leaders. (Check out my YouTube channel for three-minute videos of my athletic adventures that will offer insight and challenge you to be a better leader: bit.ly/CoachJulieComptonYouTube).

At the risk of alienating those outside the USA, let's look at strategy through the lens of an American football team. Although I haven't played football myself, even a simplistic view can shed a light on strategy. The team itself has to have skillful players; that is the talent. The coaches, who are the leaders, need to understand not only the game but the competition. Coaches have to practice with the team consistently for perfect execution. Winning the game is not only about execution, but the overall strategy for the game. Strategies could be to run the ball versus throw the ball, or to use certain plays at specific times. It even involves determining when to reveal a play so that only certain opponents in the season will see certain plays.

Liz Wiseman and Greg McKeown, in their book *Multipliers*, discussed the need for leaders to provide an atmosphere for debate.[14] I have seen executives unwilling to challenge the status quo for many reasons, including challenges in the boardroom, pushback from peers, and pressure from promises made to shareholders. This can lead to falling behind the competition or a false, inflated belief in their success. Leaders must always stay attuned and open to data that people have to share and listen to the quietest voice in the room. Seek out input and be known as a leader who encourages healthy debate.

When mistakes are made, pick up and clean up fast and move on quickly to the next competitive position. Indecisiveness is the same as having no strategy. Once the strategy is agreed upon, revisit it often because the landscape can change in the blink of an eye.

The lightning pace of global business and the number of new startups every day can sneak up in your rearview mirror. Competitors can and will pass you in a flash, so don't take successes for granted. Just look at current business examples such as Amazon and the marketplaces it has entered: retail, bookstores, commercial real estate, transportation, groceries, and in 2018 they mentioned joining Warren Buffett in some form of health care.[15] Jeff Bezos, Amazon CEO, has been vocal about Amazon's vision to sell everything to everyone everywhere.[16] What a goal!

And it looks like he is succeeding to date with his vision and supporting strategy.

Even if you aren't at the top levels of an organization, *every* leader has some area(s) in which they could be more strategic. A client of mine who was a newer leader working in the pharmaceutical industry once asked me, "Why should I be strategic when I am not in a position that determines the direction of the company?" Her manager had added into her development plan the need to be more strategic in her role. Once we began to discuss her perspective and workload, she gained insight into how she was accountable for positioning certain work and the impact it had on other departments. When that clicked, she began to look at different strategies to accomplish her team's work. She could connect what she was doing with the greater "why" of the company.

Strategy is important, and every company has a strategic deck to show it. Being armed with the best strategy is not a guarantee you will be successful. As Tim Armstrong said, "People spend 90 percent of their time on the strategy and 10 percent of the time on people. My guess is if you reversed that you might have a better outcome."[17]

Coaching Challenge:

As your coach, I challenge you to do the following:

1. Revisit your strategy every three to six months. Look at external factors, competition, trends, customers, markets, technology, labor, politics, and the economy.

2. Check the pulse of your organization or team to see how the strategies are being executed at all levels.

3. What is your strategic development process? Are the right people involved?

4. How are you monitoring your culture? How can you make it both top-down and bottom-up?

5. Read one of the numerous books on strategy by Michael E. Porter.

12. What Got Me Here

*"There are few things more powerful than a
life lived with passionate clarity."*
—Erwin McManus

FRANKLY, IT TOOK A little longer than I thought to lead
our company through the major transformation and disruption, but it worked! My big risk paid off. Not exactly
how I thought it would, mind you, but it was successful.
It took almost three years to execute the strategic play I
envisioned with the executives back on that cold January
day. I left the company soon after we'd hit our revenue
goal, because I knew there was still no room for me to
have an executive role there. It didn't take long for re-
cruiters in my industry to offer me a CEO position with a
smaller organization due to my highly publicized success
with the product I had pushed. Now I find myself stand-
ing backstage inside a beautiful ballroom, about to give an
acceptance speech in front of 2,000 or so business people
for being recognized as one of the top influential female

CEOs of the year. I feel humbled to be here, and again, unsure I deserve this reward.

"Please give a warm welcome to Dianne Gableton." That's my cue. Time to give my first major speech as a CEO receiving an award. When I took my first job, I had no idea I would be so inspired to make it this far in my career. As I walk out on stage, I have a flashback to graduation: the eager girl that I was, too good for most jobs and yet green as could be. I attribute my success to my mentors, the calculated risks I took, the teams who worked so hard with me, and mostly to a character trait my parents instilled in me—resilience. That's what I want to talk about in my acceptance speech. I feel a duty to pass on to others what I have learned. I want to encourage others to find their inner strength as leaders—to persevere through setbacks and learn from mistakes, and always, always, go for your dreams.

My success as a leader is grounded in continuously learning and applying new skills, along with being deeply self-aware. I am 42 years old and thrilled to be where I stand. I am not sure where my career will go from here, but no matter what, I will be looking for insights to learn and share with others!

I begin . . . "Ladies and Gentlemen, I am honored to receive this award and humbled to imagine I am on this list with these other distinguished female CEOs."

Author's Closing Thoughts

I AGREE WITH JOHN Kotter, top leadership guru, who made a prediction years ago in his book *Leading Change*, which has come true: "The rate of change is not going to slow down anytime soon. If anything, competition in most industries will probably speed up even more in the next few decades."[18] Given our VUCA world, along with technological advances, we need approaches that will help our leaders to navigate and succeed.

I believe the only way to lead for the future is through clarity of purpose, curiosity of others, organizational focus and alignment, agility, and self-reflection. If companies and their leaders strive to succeed in these areas, they will rise to the top. To do that, we need leaders who are humble, open-minded, inclusive, confident, vulnerable, and reflective.

Human beings have one thing over the digital world—we can actually connect with each other in a heartfelt way. I only hope we, as a society, remember this while advancing on the business and technology front.

I wish you success in your journey as a leader and encourage you to constantly look for insights along the way and pass them on to others.

If you enjoyed this book, please tell others and consider leaving an honest review on Amazon. I would love for you to connect with me:

LinkedIn: linkedin.com/in/juliecomptonphd

YouTube: bit.ly/CoachJulieComptonYouTube

My website: www.comptoncoaching.com

Recommended Reading

Blanchard, Kenneth H., Patricia Zigarmi, and Drea Zigarmi. *Leadership and the One Minute Manager: Increasing Effectiveness through Situational Leadership.* New York: William Morrow, an Imprint of HarperCollins, 2013.

Bradbery, Travis, and Jean Greaves. *Emotional Intelligence 2.0.* San Diego: TalentSmart, 2009.

Chapman, Gary. *The Five Love Languages.* Chicago: Northfield Publishing, 2015.

Crane, Thomas. *The Rise of the Coaching Leader.* San Diego: FTA Press, 2018.

Goldsmith, Marshall, and Mark Reiter. *Triggers: Creating Behaviors that Last—Becoming the Person You Want to Be.* New York: Crown Publishing, 2015.

Harkins, Phil. *Powerful Conversations: How High Impact Leaders Communicate.* New York: McGraw Hill Education, 2017.

Kotter, John P. *Leading Change*. Boston: Harvard Business Press, 2012.

Lencioni, Patrick. *The Five Dysfunctions of a Team: A Leadership Fable*. San Francisco: Josey–Bass, 2002.

McKeown, Greg. *Essentialism. The Disciplined Pursuit of Less*. New York: Crown Business, 2014.

Moore, Margaret, Edward Phillips, and John Hanc. *Organize Your Emotions, Optimize Your Life*. New York: Harper Audio, 2016.

Ogwell, D. "Stakeholder Management." Paper presented at PMI Global Congress 2003—EMEA, The Hague, South Holland, The Netherlands. Newtown Square, PA: Project Management Institute, 2003.

Rath, Tom. *Strengths Finder 2.0*. New York: Gallup Press, 2007.

Schein, Edgar H. *Humble Inquiry: The Gentle Art of Asking Instead of Telling*. San Francisco: Berrett-Koehler Publishers, 2013.

Sinek, Simon. *Start with Why: How Great Leaders Inspire Everyone to Take Action*. New York: Penguin Books, 2011.

Stanier, Michael Bungay. *The Coaching Habit: Say Less, Ask More and Change the Way You Lead Forever*. Toronto: Box of Crayons Press, 2016.

Wiseman, Liz, and Greg McKeown. *Multipliers: How the Best Leaders Make Everyone Smarter.* New York: Harper Business, 2010.

Endnotes

1 Linda Adams, "Learning a New Skill Is Easier Said than Done," Gordon Training International, accessed September 5, 2018, http://www.gordontraining.com/free-workplace-articles/learning-a-new-skill-is-easier-said-than-done/.

2 Daniel Goleman, *Emotional Intelligence: Why It Can Matter More Than IQ* (New York: Bantam Bell, 1995).

3 Susan Tardanico, "Five Steps to Increase Your Influence," *Forbes*, December 21, 2011, https://www.forbes.com/sites/work-in-progress/2011/12/21/five-steps-to-increase-your-influence/#7e882d66372c.

4 i4cp, "You Want It When?," press release, June 26, 2007, https://www.i4cp.com/news/2007/06/26/you-want-it-when.

5 Brian Tracy, "How to Delegate the Right Tasks to the Right People: Effective Management Skills for Leadership Success," (blog), Brian Tracy International, accessed September 18, 2018, https://www.briantracy.com/blog/leadership-success/how-to-delegate-the-right-tasks-to-the-right-people-effective-management-skills-for-leadership-success/.

6 Greg McKeown, *Essentialism: The Disciplined Pursuit of Less* (New York: Crown Business, 2014).

7 Andrew Sumitani, "The Ultimate Guide to Employee Engagement," (blog) TinyPulse, August 17, 2018, https://www.tinypulse.com/blog/guide-to-employee-engagement.

8   Stephen Covey, *Seven Habits of Highly Effective People* (New York: FranklinCovey, Simon and Schuster, 2013).

9   Edgar H. Schein, *Humble Inquiry: The Gentle Art of Asking Instead of Telling* (San Francisco: Berrett-Koehler, 2013).

10 S. S. Crandell et al., "The Trillion-Dollar Difference" (Los Angeles: Korn Ferry Institute, 2016).

11 John Whitmore, *Coaching for Performance: GROWing Human Potential and Purpose—The Principles and Practice of Coaching and Leadership* (Boston: Nicholas Brealey, 2009).

12 John P. Kotter, *Leading Change* (Boston: Harvard Business Press, 2012).

13 Christopher Vollmer and Daniel Gross, "Oath CEO Tim Armstrong Believes in the Promise of the Mobile Consumer," *Strategy+Business*, 92 (Autumn 2018), https://www.strategy-business.com/article/Oath-CEO-Tim-Armstrong-Believes-in-the-Promise-of-the-Mobile-Consumer.

14 Liz Wiseman and Greg McKeown, *Multipliers: How the Best Leaders Make Everyone Smarter* (New York: HarperCollins Business, 2010).

15 Lydia Ramsey, "Warren Buffet Has Been Speaking Out about the Cost of Healthcare for Years," *Business Insider*, January 30, 2018, https://finance.yahoo.com/news/warren-buffett-speaking-cost-healthcare-201642279.html.

16 Jeff Bezos, interview by Charlie Rose, *60 Minutes*, December 1, 2013, https://www.cbsnews.com/news/amazons-jeff-bezos-looks-to-the-future/.

17 Vollmer and Gross, "Oath CEO Tim Armstrong."

18 Kotter, *Leading Change*.

Acknowledgments

Thanks to:

All of my clients over the last 20 years, thank you for giving me the gift of helping you be the leader you desire to be and teaching me along the way. I love what I do and so appreciate you!

My parents, Merritt and Bette, for their love, support, and continuous listening ear over the years.

Dianne Reynolds, for sharing her inspiring Kauai home where it all began. Adam Sugarman, who said, "Just write something."

Steve Moore, who believed in my creativity.

Laurie-Ann Murabito, for your endless support and friendship—I finished this because of you!

My amazing colleagues I have worked with and learned from over the years (you know who you are).

My editor, Kim Foster, who is a delight to work with.

My friends Steve C., Bill B.,Sam W., and Angie, who inspired me to "get this done," Larry for always being there for me, as well as the numerous outdoor adventure friends who cheered me on.

And I thank you, God, for your Spirit, love, and guidance for this book, which I hope will have a positive impact on everyone who reads it.

About the Author

DR. JULIE COMPTON IS a highly sought-after executive coach who launched her company in the 1990s to partner with organizations to strengthen their leadership talent through coaching and facilitation. Her primary focus is on coaching Executives, VPs, and Sr. Directors. Julie helps clients become more aware of their style, leverage their strengths, and build their capabilities in many aspects of leadership development, including emotional intelligence, strategic thinking, influencing, stakeholder relationships, communication, and empowering teams.

Julie's coaching approach is practical, methodical, action-oriented, and customized to each individual. Her clients come from numerous industries, including retail, biotech, pharma, O&G, high tech, financial, government, and health care. She has a PhD in Adult and Organizational Learning and prior experience in business and academia.

Julie is also an athlete and uses her adventures as analogies for leadership and encourages leaders to change through videos, blogs, and articles. She creates informative three-minute outside adventure videos to challenge leaders.

Subscribe to her channel on YouTube (bit.ly.CoachJulie ComptonYouTube), and sign up for her articles on LinkedIn (linkedin/in/juliecomptonphd) or go to her website (www.comptoncoaching.com) for information on her coaching services and her leadership blog.

CPSIA information can be obtained
at www.ICGtesting.com
Printed in the USA
LVHW040431100320
649437LV00006B/943